# **Dirty Talk**

What to Say During Sex To Please, Tease, and Drive Him Crazy—A Guide to Sexting, Phone Conversations and More

*(To Get You Started Sparking Your Sexual Life: Inspiring Examples That Will Astound Your Partner In Bed)*

**Adrian Plourde**

# TABLE OF CONTENT

The Skill Of Being Alert ......................................................... 1

The Real Story Behind Women's Controversial Views ........................................................................................ 7

Enhancing Your Ability To Communicate ................... 19

How To Spot Inappropriate Conduct Before It Ruins Your Relationship ................................................................. 33

Adult Sexting ............................................................................ 60

Dirty Talk Inspiration: Where To Find The Juiciest Ideas ........................................................................................... 78

Tips For Tantric Intimacy .................................................... 97

The Fundamentals Of Sexual Education .................. 140

## The Skill Of Being Alert

Dears, pay attention! Being alert is the key that opens the door to men's hearts if you want to know how to draw them in and keep them captivated by your amazingness!

Now, don't get me wrong—it's important to pursue your passions and interests. However, paying close attention to your partner's hobbies can go a long way toward demonstrating to him your sincere concern and curiosity about what drives him.

The good news is that if you're not into basketball, you don't have to become an ardent supporter of your favorite team to be attentive. It also doesn't imply that you must take up all of his interests. We're not discussing vanishing into his reality. It all comes down to establishing a rapport with him on his territory.

So, how do you maintain a man's undying love for you and make sure your partnership doesn't smoke? My dears, it's as easy as it gets. Start observing his hobbies and posing inquiries. He shows sincere interest and zeal when he discusses his passions. This simple gesture of attention will make him feel noticed and valued, and I promise he will be happy to repay the favor.

For instance, acknowledge and congratulate him on his stylish new haircut. Inquire about his hobbies, accomplishments of late, and the book he's been reading. He will experience a strong sense of connection and know that you appreciate him as a unique person when you talk to him about these topics.

But remember that being attentive involves more than just asking questions and listening; it also entails actively engaging with his environment. Even if they are not your first choice, join him in what he enjoys doing. This indicates that you're willing to put in the effort to share experiences, but it doesn't mean you have to give up your interests and pastimes.

If he's a big sports fan, I propose taking him to a game or throwing a watch party for his buddies. If he enjoys hiking, consider taking him on a weekend trip to see a beautiful trail. You may strengthen your relationship and create memories by getting involved in his interests.

Supporting his aspirations is another facet of being observant. Urge him to follow his passions and be there for him when he does. Your confidence in his skills and your steadfast support will motivate him to aim high, whether his goals are to launch a new company, study a musical instrument, or prepare for a marathon.

Recall that being attentive is an art that involves more than meets the eye.

Observe the small details that hold significance for him. Give him a present demonstrating your thoughtfulness, or surprise him with his favorite food. These actions show that you genuinely care about him and know his needs and wants.

In summation, concentration is necessary to win and maintain his heart. You will establish a strong emotional bond and maintain the flames of love by being curious, actively engaging in his environment, supporting his objectives, and being mindful of the small things. Thus, darlings, embrace the power of focus and watch your partnership blossom!

## The Real Story Behind Women's Controversial Views

What are a woman's enticing weapons? How can they subjugate a man? Gaining an understanding of the strategies women employ in passive seduction will help you better comprehend the dynamics between men and women.

From what a buddy of mine at SeduzionePratica informed me:

"I wear a low-cut shirt and seduce a man by flashing him my tits as soon as I get the chance. I make excuses like "Oh, I got soiled here," and lean towards him. I make sure he's observing me as I display the merchandise. To entice him sexually and make him look is the exact aim.

I charmed them all and even used the same tactic to gain benefits at the establishments where I provide drinks or the stores where I receive discounts.

I know that when a man is completely enamored, he loses all sense of reason and assumes the appearance of a boiled fish. I kept bragging till I got this response.

I tell him, "Ooh where are you looking?" when I see that he is staring at my tits. I intentionally bitch to show him what kind of person he is. I left him wondering, leading him to believe that "I want to do this with her, even though she didn't show me the boobs voluntarily."

I don't want someone who acts only once they are positive I am present; therefore, I treat him like garbage after that. I want a man to take me just when I seem to be absent from his life through my words.

It must occur to him that the very fact that I remain there and continue to speak with him is of interest to me.

If he's not present, I need to make the bitch and accuse him of coming out of it a winner, even though they are fake words of rejection. I can always tell myself and him, "Look, I wasn't trying with you, I never wanted you, I'm even telling you!" if he were to say, "I'm sorry, but I'm engaged."

I want to convince him that he is my suitor and that I am ready to decide. I'll make him think he deserves all the glory when we're in bed, even though it all began with me picking out what to wear to leave the house.

Every woman has advantages; she only needs to show them off a little. When something doesn't work, you'll know it right away. He will hang from your lips and do everything for you, including cocktails, benefits, and gifts, when you put on the miniskirt or just the leggings and bend for a little while. However, he is unaware that he will never have you in that manner. The only way to get close to a veiled woman is to playfully challenge her, to go past her snarky demeanor and her "f*ck you want?"

We wouldn't be together now if my lover hadn't kissed me when we first met, disregarding my dissatisfied remarks.

Whoa, fascinating, huh?

She will launch the bait, and you must act by the game rules rather than biting like a "boiled fish" to win. The bold guy with the confidence to pursue his goals despite "obstacles" is the handsome man.

How can you determine whether she truly meant to provoke you with the indication she provided? Simply put, it's time to move if she tells you anything like, "The f*ck are you staring at?" and keeps chatting to you while sending you signals of interest with her body.

However, if she tells you that you are going to hell, gets up, and leaves, then lets go, then it was a clear NO.

Dirty Talk: Crucial Dos and Don'ts in Chapter Four

We can obtain extremely vital information from women's publications and blogs unavailable elsewhere. We present concepts and viewpoints that aid in understanding, coping, or satisfying them. When they try to talk nasty for the first few times, many women still experience embarrassment.

Even if your partner shares your desire for obscene language, someone has to initiate contact. Living it up in the bedroom isn't difficult; you simply need a few pointers. You won't find the vulgar talk useful, so here are a few dos.

**The Shoulds:** Inform him of its size. Guys are complementary narcissists. Make his body, abilities, and results feel fantastic. This should be consistent with his responsibilities. You should advise him on how to please you and get you to feel more soiled in conversation.

Before getting into bed, you must create your sexual confidence, just like anything else. Wordplay, pre-play flirtation, and sex are all examples of it. One advantage is that it establishes the future's cadence and tone.

Telling your guy how you feel is the easiest method to initiate a natural dirty chat. A smart place to start would be by telling him how amazing you feel on the inside.

Dirty conversation can take many different forms. that might be as simple as "Yes!" or more complex like "I feel so good!" or "Yes, I really love it!" But stupidity relies on how honest and liberated you and your spouse are. Even if it takes effort, you can finally establish trust.

Don't overdo it or strive too hard. Avoid going overboard. Although the porn stars you watch could look real, the atmosphere is ruined if you yell all of the profane words you can think of. Being straightforward but casual is preferable to upsetting the atmosphere.

If it isn't your friend, don't continue. Before pre-playing, here, wordplay and sex are crucial. You can tell if your partner is complying or not.

Recognize what dirty speech is; perhaps you require an eBook or other guide containing all the information you require on dirty talk. Look around for the finest how-to book that will lead you from the beginning to using foul language.

No one has ever engaged in dirty language during a sexual encounter before. Few of us do, even though most wish to attempt it—even just fantasize about it.

We all know that having sex is an adventure, but if couples don't push the boundaries, it can become boring and routine. Your sexual life will improve with dirty language, but there are some important things you may and cannot do to maintain the significance of the experience.

You can't reignite things until you try, even though your companion may want to talk as filthy as you do. You should begin cautiously and refrain from just screaming the first inappropriate thing that comes to mind.

It's ideal to begin by softly whispering what you'd like him to say or do in your partner's ear, then watch for his response. It will be interpreted as a cue to speak or act. It's always a little difficult the first time, but eventually, one of you will step up and roll the ball.

For a few months, consider the thought of dirty chatting as you get to know your partner and their preferences.

In the third month of our marriage, I suggested that I talk to my partner sexually, and to my amazement, he was exactly the kind of person I expected. On your first date, avoid engaging in obscene conversation as it may turn off some people and be blatantly impolite.

It takes practice to become an expert at nasty talk. You can only know what your partner wants to hear, what words or phrases bother him or her, and what physical actions should come after your conversations. All of these things come from experience.

It's also critical to keep in mind that not everyone enjoys having sex with someone who talks nasty. Once, my friend Lisa, a reserved Christian man, told me that she tried to speak to her husband in bed to lighten the mood, but it had the opposite effect and made him lose his erection right away.

It resulted in an unpleasant situation and the needless disparaging phrase being used about it. The claim is that you must know who you are talking to and have the confidence to know whether or not you are being nasty talkative.

## Enhancing Your Ability To Communicate

Building solid connections and enticing women both require effective communication. We establish connections, trust, and understanding with people through conversation. A person with strong communication abilities can draw in ladies in several ways.

Methods for Developing Strong Communication Abilities

Building solid connections and enticing women both require effective communication. We establish connections, trust, and understanding with people through conversation. A person with strong communication abilities can draw in ladies in several ways.

This is listening carefully to what women have to say and reacting in a way that conveys your appreciation for and understanding of their viewpoint. Active listening to women can help you better understand and establish a connection with them by providing you with insight into their feelings and thoughts.

2. Establishing connection and trust requires openness and honesty in communication. Building trust and a connection with the woman you are attempting to attract can be facilitated by being forthright and honest about your ideas and feelings.

3. It's critical to communicate confidently since it demonstrates your ability to express yourself clearly and that you are at ease in your skin. Communicating with confidence can attract women and foster deeper relationships.

4. Connecting with women and making them feel at ease can be achieved through humor in conversation. Laughter can provide a positive first impression and break the ice.

5. Being forceful in conversation is crucial since it demonstrates your ability to speak up for what's right and effectively express yourself. By projecting confidence and being straightforward in your approach, being

aggressive in communication can help you draw in ladies.

How to Draw a Woman in with Your Body Language

In addition to being a crucial communication component, body language may be quite effective in luring a woman.

Maintain Eye Contact

Establishing eye contact is a potent technique to express attraction and interest. Establishing eye contact with a woman might convey your confidence and interest in her thoughts.

Grin

One of the most appealing things about a person is their sincere grin. Frequently grinning and displaying friendliness and approachability might leave a good impression on a woman.

Explicit body language

Being friendly and eager to get to know the woman can be conveyed through open body language, which includes facing her, keeping your distance, and holding out your arms.

Position

It is possible to convey confidence and self-assurance by keeping your posture straight and standing up straight. Additionally, it can give you a taller, more appealing appearance.

Feel

Touch is a potent tool for establishing rapport and expressing interest. You might express your interest in a woman by gently and respectfully touching her arm or shoulder.

Reflection

Being able to subtly copy someone else's body language is known as mirrored movement. Mirroring a woman's body language might be a good way to establish interest and a relationship.

Remember that nonverbal cues like body language should be employed in addition to spoken communication. Always show the individual you're trying to attract your respect and consent.

How to Talk to Women

Although approaching a lady can be intimidating, it can also be a good and enjoyable experience if you have the correct attitude and strategy.

Methods for Talking to Women in Different Social Contexts

Have Self-Assurance

The secret to approaching a woman is confidence. Possessing confidence increases your chances of striking up a conversation and making a positive first impression. Make sure to smile, make eye contact, and stand erect when approaching a woman. Demonstrate to her your self-assurance and curiosity in getting to know her.

Show reverence.

When interacting with women, respect is essential. Always consider her body language and respect her personal space and limits. If she appears uneasy or disinterested, accept her choice and go on.

Make a Positive First Observation

Making a good first impression is crucial, so make sure you look well. Be well-groomed, dress nicely, wear a nice scent, and practice good hygiene. When approaching a woman, pay attention to how you look and try to look as professional as possible.

Employ open-ended inquiries:

It's crucial to have a conversation starter when you approach a woman. One excellent technique to get a conversation started and going is using open-ended inquiries. Inquire about her hobbies, interests, and employment. Asking yes-or-no questions will usually result in brief and boring interactions, so steer clear of them.

Discover points of agreement.

Creating a relationship with the woman you are approaching can be facilitated by finding areas of agreement. Seek for shared hobbies or interests and utilize them to discuss. Whether you both enjoy hiking, for instance, you can find out which hiking routes she likes to use or whether she plans to trek this weekend.

Be Sincere

Be sincere and true to who you are. Refrain from trying to pass for someone you're not and from trying to win her over with made-up or exaggerated tales. She will feel more at ease with you and trust you more if you are sincere.

### Pay Attention To Her Reactions

Throughout the chat, pay attention to her body language and replies. If she displays signs of worry or disinterest, acknowledge her feelings and move on. Don't try to force the conversation to go on or be forceful.

### Be Your Person

Always stay true to yourself when interacting with women. Be loyal, sincere, and true to who you are. Being authentic can help you feel more at ease during the conversation, increasing the likelihood that the woman will be curious to learn more about you.

## How to Strike Up a Discussion with Any Woman and Keep It Going

### Get Ready

It's crucial to be ready before approaching a woman. To develop a conversation opener, you may look up current events online or glance at her profile if you're on a platform. For instance, you may inquire about her favorite pastime or whether she is aware of the recently approved legislation. Being ready for the talk will make you feel more at ease and confident.

Establish a Relationship

Look for a common ground to establish a connection with the woman when you start a conversation. One way to strike up a conversation is to discuss a popular TV show you both watch or comment about the weather. Establishing a common ground will facilitate the establishment of a connection and improve the flow of the conversation.

Display Interest

Actively listen to the woman and express interest in her words. For instance, if she tells you that she is a nurse, find out what motivated her to pursue that line of work. Seek to understand her on a true level by posing open-ended inquiries. Maintaining the flow of the conversation and avoiding it from becoming one-sided will require showing attention.

Do Not Hold Awkward Quiet

There should never be an awkward silence if you want the conversation to continue. For instance, attempt to refocus the conversation by posing a fresh query or offering a comment when there is a pause. You may find out what she has planned for the weekend or whether she has visited any fascinating areas lately.

Be Truthful

Always stay true to yourself when conversing. You'll feel more at ease and relaxed if you are sincere and authentic, which will help the discussion flow more easily. For instance, be honest and true to yourself; don't overstate your accomplishments or pretend to be someone you're not.

Avert Contentious Subjects

Steer clear of contentious or delicate subjects that could elicit defensiveness or discomfort from the woman. For instance, don't talk about religion, politics, or delicate personal matters. Maintain a lighthearted and impartial conversational tone to ensure seamless communication. For instance, See Her Responses.

For instance, it's better to depart with a courteous apology if she doesn't appear interested in talking to you or doesn't answer your queries. You may be uninteresting and not using the appropriate dating strategies.

## How To Spot Inappropriate Conduct Before It Ruins Your Relationship

Did you know that occasionally, there can be "poor sex" in healthy relationships?

It's possible that having sex is just enjoyable. It is, nonetheless, essential to a happy marriage.

Great sex can be detrimental to a healthy relationship, just as it can maintain the "spark" in one.

Neglecting one another's sexual activity and seeing it as "no big deal" can have detrimental effects on a strong and happy marriage.

Bad sex may damage your relationship in four ways.

❖ Unhealthy sex reduces communication between you and your partner.

People converse with one another during sex. What they want, don't want, how they want it, etc.

As a result, both couples might become closer and more intimate.

When problems start to arise in the bedroom, what happens next?

One study suggests that fewer sexual exchanges in the bedroom could lead to fewer conversations overall.

Reduced communication could be detrimental to your relationship.

Reduced communication makes both parties more aloof, harming the partnership or, in the worst cases, forcing it to end.

- ❖ Have bad sex to make you more irritable.

After having inadequate and disappointing sex, both parties could feel under pressure and unsatisfied.

Making rational decisions is more challenging when one is frustrated.

You can become incapable of taking a joke, lose your sense of humor, and overreact to little things.

This makes it more likely that you and your partner may miscommunicate, leading to more disagreements and strain on your relationship.

Horrible sex can cause difficulties that impact not only your relationship but also other areas of your life.

❖ Negative sex does not initiate a desire for sex.

When you have unpleasant sex in a relationship, your desire for sex may drop.

Your wants are all focused on activities you can accomplish alone, not on spending quality time with your partner.

It is common to not desire sex all the time or not want sex at the same time.

But if you never want to have sex, this can be a problem.

When the desire to have sex with your partner fades, your frequent bad sex with them may be a contributing factor in the decline.

A happy relationship involves a lot of sex.

For some people, having sex is the best way to emotionally connect with their spouse.

Furthermore, when bad sex makes a partner no longer want to have sex, it is difficult for both partners to keep the essential connection in a relationship.

Lack of desire for sex, or even mismatched desire, causes couples to drift apart and ultimately leads to the dissolution of the union.

❖ Ineffective sex ruins the passion and emotions in a partnership.

In the same way that good sex revitalizes a relationship, bad sex can smother feelings inside it.

Sex creates an emotional bond between you and your partner; if that bond is broken, it could be challenging for your feelings to develop further and for your relationship to progress.

Satisfied sex keeps a relationship's "fire" burning.

However, having insufficient sex could put out the "fire" in your partnership.

If your sex is horrible, you might not feel the need to do the things you enjoy doing with your partner.

Not spending as much time together as you used to causes the distance between you two to widen, which may finally cause your relationship to fail.

Section Six

Examine the Resources Used in the Child's Education

Overview

In the modern world, practically all organizations and educational institutions offer students a sexual education curriculum. You must be aware of the materials your child is being taught as a responsible parent, particularly when they are in the classroom's four corners.

When they hear the term "sex," some individuals feel uneasy and confused. It's critical to find out what is being taught in your child's classroom when you notice they are going through something similar, especially at school.

The Details of the Materials Being Taught in Schools

These days, most educational institutions use sex education books, also available online and in stores. Most sex education books contain comprehensive instructions that can help you learn a lot about sexuality.

Increasing your child's sexual awareness is one of the primary goals of sex education programs offered in the majority of establishments and educational institutions.

The majority of sex education literature recommends that you start having conversations with your child about sex before they start acting sexually.

Sexual education programs are, therefore, carefully designed and developed to give your child skills and information that they may use shortly, especially when they're ready to tackle the real world of sex. The sex education programs and courses offered at universities and schools will assist your child in developing sexual orientation, safe sex, and abstinence so you can be confident in their wonderful potential for these life skills.

Furthermore, your child can get help with questions about sex from sexual health services. These sexual health programs will make it possible for your child to learn everything there is to know about sex in a secure and comfortable environment.

Male Sexual Expectations

These are the 20 Things Men Want From Their Partners in Sexual Activity.

1. He wants you to express your preferences to him.

Males learn best through observation. Use your gestures to convey to him how you feel about it. Laying on the bed and touching yourself while telling him to gaze but not touch is a sexy role-playing technique. Vanessa Geffrard, spokesman for Lovers, an adult health brand and retailer, says, "Don't be scared to move your hands, position your body, and use verbal and nonverbal communication to create a nice time for you both." An enticing, sensual way of expressing and demonstrating).

2. He wants to remove it from the bedroom.

Men are fond of variety. The COO of Inquisitive Fox, a network for people who are interested in polyamory, and a sex expert, Jacqueline Misla, suggests finding different places to play, such as the laundry room, kitchen table, car, or even outside, to keep things exciting. "Having sex in unfamiliar places can also result in more enjoyable and imaginative role-playing chances."

3. He wants you to give him a direct glance.

Yes, there are instances in which having an "emotional connection" is crucial. According to relationship expert Chloe Ballatore, guys are curious about their partners' emotions and reactions to their behavior. Women should be able to relish what their boyfriend does for and with them.

4. He's itching for more! Laughing

Humor relieves the tension of, well, everything. The same applies to sexual connections. "I've been in relationships and encounters where the bedroom is the center of everything for years. It's like when we throw away our clothing, our sense of humor goes with them," Bryan T., 28, adds. "Living nearby and releasing some of the pressure I feel to perform can both be enhanced by laughter. This makes it simpler to be impulsive and have fun," he says.

5. He wants to "make love" too.

Of course, having sex is good, but so is getting to know someone better on a physical level. Although men don't always bring up the subject of "making love," sexologist and therapist Shamyra asserts that they typically do so after their significant other has. According to Shamyra, these men want to "make love," which she describes as engaging in more leisurely, thoughtful, and intense sexual activity. She claims they have triumphed against the shame attached to the cliched nature of the term "making love."

6. now and again, he wants you to lead.

One of the most common complaints Shamyra hears from clients in couples counseling is that male partners in heterosexual relationships occasionally feel like they have to start the conversation when it comes to their female counterparts. Shamyra, "Men like to be enticed; they like to feel desired and desirable." "Starting sex offers your boyfriend a huge confidence boost since it lets him know you want him," according to the writer.

As a hint, find out how he would like you to initiate a conversation. Furthermore, tell him what you're doing if you're trying to get him to start having sex with you by doing things like petting his back.

7. he wants you to be boisterous if you feel like it.

They are erotic music that truly turns on men, so they love to hear it. Not to mention that it frees you as well. If you're feeling it right now, don't hold back; it's just like communicating, but sexier. Says Shamyra, "Shout if you're a screamer. Don't hold back your grunts, groans, yells, and growls of delight."

8. He wants you to take an active part.

Shamyra states that "many men prefer to have sex with women who actively participate." To actively participate, simply respond to his thrusts with your own, grind your hips, and flex your PC muscles (the muscles that extend from your pubic bone to your tailbone). You can accomplish all of these from where you are right now.

Squeezing his arms and pulling his body into you with your hands are other ways to express your enjoyment of the motion to your partner.

9. He wants you to talk to him.

This has two implications: first, he must tell you what he wants. Secondly, having a partner who can express their preferences for physical contact is incredibly alluring and allows him to be somewhat sincere.

10. He wants to be in different roles.

Humans crave novelty, which is partly why something like hotel sex is so damn alluring. No one is advising you to step outside your comfort zone to win over a guy, but hey, if the thought occurs to you that it could be sexy to have him turn you around and bone you from behind against your kitchen counter, then go for it. If you and your spouse spend a few nights a week doing it missionary in bed, you both probably want something new occasionally.

11. He wants you to be the boss sometimes.

Suppose you think of sexual activity as a group project, and you are committed to getting an A (or having an orgasm). In that case, your group members may be talkative, but if you want to succeed and it's 3 a.m. the night before an assignment is due, you might have to take the lead.

Take the lead, show your partner how you escape alone, and tell him about your dreams. He will love the idea of having his peep show and find out what you need to get off. After all, you are effectively purchasing future climaxes.

12. Tell it as it is with him.

Nobody has ever wanted for *less* direction in bed, even though he might have everything under control. Save the uncertainty for sexting, and don't be afraid to voice your actual wants.

Don't be afraid to tell him, "Ehh, that's not doing anything for me," but you may also say, "I enjoyed it when you were doing this earlier." Always use positive reinforcement when training. Just emphasize the positives while letting him know what you are and aren't into. Trust us, you won't offend him.

Specializing in sex therapy, Gloria Brame, Ph.D., of Georgia, says, "Tell him how nice it feels when he does something well or reminds him of a method that always gets you off." If he doesn't provide enough foreplay, ask him to warm you up with his hand or mouth and explain that you want to prolong the experience.

13. He desires to view every detail.

Tyler, 21, remembers, "One day during sex, my girlfriend walked me to a mirror so we could see ourselves in action." I thought that was incredibly sexy, but how into it she seemed made it much sexier. Men always prefer what they see to what they receive, so if you're experiencing it too, show him your eyes.

14. He wants your sexual tastes to feel natural to you.

As Brame notes, women often hesitate to act inappropriately when dating because they don't want to ruin his perception of them as a "nice girlfriend" or make him think they're odd. However, men want to see your raw side but don't want to ask since they don't want to hurt your feelings. The best way to connect "in bed" is to be open about what you want, despite your concerns about what other people might think. Be proud that you've always wanted to share the cost of bed shackles or that he might find it "strange" that you need a vibrator to get off.

## Make Use of Authentic Teaching Methods

As I've mentioned before, authentic teaching is incredibly effective in teaching students about sex and sexuality. As parents, we have a responsibility to do everything in our power to teach our children what love, respect, and trust are, and one way to do this is by incorporating authentic teaching techniques into our lesson plans. Let's look at some of the ways that we could use authentic teaching:

### Maintain A Journal

For a week, you and your child can keep a diary where you can write individual examples of family members demonstrating love, respect, and trust for one another. Review the journal at the end of the week and discuss why each of your entries is a good example of the big three.

Tell a Story

Let's say that two sixteen-year-old students dating for two months go to a friend's house one evening and spend time in the backyard after going to the movies. They walk over to the porch and start kissing after chatting with their friends for a little while. After a few seconds, the boy touches his girlfriend's breast for the first time; she doesn't mind at all until he tries to reach beneath her bra. The girl tries to move his hand away, but he persists. He begins to cry, but she lets it.

- Ask your child if he thinks the male could ever respect the girl, and if not, why not?
- Find out if the boy will be dependable with the female in the future, and why not?

Why shouldn't the girl go out with the boy again if not?

- What does this teach you about love, respect, and trust in the context of sex?

One person pressuring another into sexual activity must not be tolerated; if he had quit straight away, that would be a different story. The boy may later be very sorry and perhaps seek forgiveness, or he may even claim that he only did it because he loves her. You could also claim that far too many people in relationships suffer from partner abuse and that this is a significant issue in our culture. Finally, you can talk to your child about whether the girl should go out with the boy again because he was wrong and

Expand the Circle

When your child is next with you, and you are visiting family or close friends, tell them you have been talking to your child about love, respect, and trust. Tell them you and your conversation partner have discussed identifying these qualities in a couple. Ask your family or friends for examples of how they demonstrate love, respect, and trust in their relationships. Ask your child to share an example of a relationship she has seen.

Attempt role-playing.

Encourage your child to pretend that you are his child and that he is your father (or mother). Ask him to role-play what he would say about how to spot love, respect, and trust in a relationship with someone else while you are there. Be prepared to confront him with questions that refute his claims.

Creating Models

In addition to authentic instruction, modeling a loving, respectful, and trustworthy relationship for your children can have a significant impact. We can teach our children the big three as much as we want, but the greatest influence on them will come from us as parents modeling these values in our daily lives. Periodically, remind your children of how you and your partner demonstrated love, respect, or trust.

Even if you are single, there are many opportunities to demonstrate love, respect, and trust in relationships. Give examples of times when you and your children demonstrate these qualities to one another. You can see how our children will be in a great place when they reach adolescence if you can put all that we have discussed up to this point into practice. This is because of several factors, such as their perception of us as approachable, their consideration of sexual urges and how to handle them, and the importance of love, respect, and trust in a relationship. Our influence on the types of sexual behaviors our children will and will not engage in should be evident as we continue our efforts as they move through middle school and into high school.

The importance of what you're doing will become clear as we examine the issues raised in detail in the upcoming chapter and discuss how critical it is to protect against the negative aspects of sex and sexuality while embracing their positive and life-enhancing aspects.

## Adult Sexting

Sending sexually suggestive messages, images, or videos over email, text messaging, messaging apps, social media, or other digital communication channels is known as adult sexting. It's a relatively recent phenomenon that's gained popularity as digital communication platforms have grown.

Exploring and expressing one's sexual dreams and wants through adult sexting can be beneficial. It may be a potent instrument for intimacy and connection and enable people to explore their sexuality in a safe and consenting way. It may, however, also be dangerous and have negative emotional and legal repercussions.

Everybody concerned should talk about their goals, limits, and expectations. They should also know the rules and legislation for sexting in their respective states. Only two consenting adults who are of legal age should text each other.

It is crucial to safeguard oneself against possible legal ramifications by refraining from exchanging sexting communications with kids or adults without consent. Additionally, it's critical to employ security measures to guarantee that the sexting texts are kept private.

Adult sexting is a personal decision, so before you do it, think about the possible risks and repercussions. Adult sexting may be an exciting and enjoyable method to explore and express one's sexuality when done sensibly and carefully.

Individuals become so ingrained with the importance of gendered communication that they police others and themselves to keep it that way. This is particularly valid in regards to sexting. Men are expected to communicate in a more "aggressive" and forward manner, while women are expected to be more "modest" and are frequently humiliated for sexting. This kind of gendered communication can exacerbate the stigma associated with sexting and cause emotions of humiliation or shame.

It's critical to keep in mind that everyone is free to explore and express their sexuality in whatever way that makes them feel safe and at ease. People should be allowed to engage in sexting in any way that makes them feel confident and at ease, and it should always be consensual and courteous to all parties.

Chapter 4: Usual Procedures

Dirty discussion is uncomfortable for some people. Respecting and being aware of others' limits is essential. Setting and maintaining limits in your relationship is also essential. Even if you both decide to add dirty conversations and small talk to your bedroom experience, it's important to establish what is and isn't acceptable for you two.

You and your lover can decide precisely how dirty you want to get with words with the guidance of this chapter. However, before we do anything, let's examine what constitutes inappropriate phrase content.

The Things You Said in Your Dirty Words

Speaking filthy doesn't always entail using a lot of offensive language. Rather, it expresses the idea that "I am unafraid to let my true feelings show" through language. Of course, using profanity or derogatory language frequently enables us to make the desired impression. Nevertheless, this does not imply that your foul language must be offensive. "I can't wait to stroke, kiss, suck, and choke on your huge penis," for instance. Alternatively, "I want to bury my face between your warm thighs and nibble on your hard nipples." Even though these statements don't contain swear words, whispering them in your partner's ear can quickly enhance their sexual desire. Keep in mind that the objective is to increase sexual desire rather than to demonstrate your proficiency with foul language.

When you speak negatively, try to convey one or more of the following through your words:

1. Express gratitude to your partner: Praise your significant other for their

appearance, sex, bodily parts, and general skill at whatever it is they are doing to you or even to themselves. For instance, "I can stare at your tits all day," "You sexy goddess," "I totally adore your big cock," or "You're so good with your tongue."

Of course, when expressing your gratitude, you can use profanity. Sayings like "I love what you do to me with that damn dick of yours," "You're so fucking good," or "You nice little slut" are examples.

The fact is that expressing your gratitude to your partner through words or deeds is just another method of saying "I love you." However, make it clear to your spouse by your words and delivery that you are doing something different from the "conventional, socially acceptable, and appropriate" route when expressing your gratitude. Allow them to experience the raw form of your daily "I love you" statement, which comes from the very core of your soul. And by all means, use swear words if that's how you better communicate your deepest emotions!

2. Explain your feelings: How does your partner treat you? What kind of touch are they giving you? As they touch you, what sense do you experience? Which body parts are affected by the feeling? Do you want to shout, burst into tears, melt into them, explode, or just be really calm? Talk to your partner about these

emotions rather than keeping them to yourself. "That's the spot," "I feel like coming when you stroke me that way," "Keep doing that baby, it feels so good," or "I love your warm breath on my clit" are a few examples.

Putting your feelings into words lets your spouse know that you are happy with what they are doing and also saves them the trouble of figuring out what you want and don't want.

● By engaging in activities you enjoy, they can readily develop a sexual interest in you.

● By just talking to your partner about your sexual feelings, you get to connect and amplify them. ● You let your partner assist you in discovering previously undiscovered aspects of your sexuality.

3. Explain your desired course of action for your partner: Creating suspense is one of the potent benefits of talking dirty. By describing it, you can help your partner's imagination generate an imagined and possibly more intense version of what you are about to perform or wish you could do. For example, even if they might normally appreciate your touch, verbally describing how you wish to touch them heightens the feeling of your touch since they have already envisioned and felt it before you contact them. This creates anticipation and guides their mind to your touch.

Saying something as basic as "I want to kiss every part of your beautiful body" can convey exactly what you want to accomplish. And it can be as explicit and explicit as sayings like, "I'm going to caress you until your tight little pussy is dripping wet and your entire body quakes from sheer pleasure," or, "I want to suck you until you come hard for me, and then I'll swallow every bit of your warm, thick cum." Your spouse will be more imaginative and excited the more detailed you are.

4. Find out what your spouse desires: During foreplay and sex, it is crucial to consider your partner's satisfaction, regardless of whether you are adopting a submissive role. Thus, you should use

words that facilitate your partner's expression of their desires in your dirty talk. "How would you like it, slow and gentle, or fast and rough?" is one example. "Baby, my goal is to win your favor. "Tell Daddy what you want, and I'll do it," "Your wish is my fucking command," or "Tell me about your wildest dreams, and I'll make them come true" are examples of phrases that express this.

It's not only about pleasing your lover when you ask them what they want. You might also get great satisfaction from making your lover happy. Your sexual confidence might also be bolstered by witnessing your partner experience an earth-shattering orgasm as a result of anything you performed on them. In addition, you will be the object of your partner's sexual awe. You are aware that they will have long-term sexual thoughts about you. Additionally, the simplest approach to cutting out the guesswork and doing exactly what makes them happy is to ask them what they want.

During sex, you don't always have to comply with everything your partner requests, especially if it makes you feel uneasy. However, you may get to the bottom of their sexual urges by just questioning them. It serves as a release.

It is imperative to keep in mind that your partner's sexual preferences are not to be used as a basis for criticism or assessment of their moral qualities. You run the risk of emotionally cutting yourself off from them if you ever use their fantasies or deepest sexual desires against them in a dispute.

5. Express your desires to your partner: It's not only about satisfying your lover when you talk dirty. It's also about indulging in as much sexual stimulation and pleasure as possible for oneself. Many women have allowed themselves to be misled into believing that having dirty language is solely about getting their boyfriend to like them. "To prolong his life, let me give him a manly peck on the ego." The authenticity is taken away when one approaches nasty discourse from this angle. All you are doing is reciting something you have read

somewhere or performing a script. Whether we are men or women, we all have desires. Yes, for the reasons we covered in Chapter 2 previously, men are more promiscuous. That does not, however, lessen a woman's desire for sex.

Conversely, some men might find it hard to express their most intense sexual desires to their spouse. They don't want to come across to their spouse as petty, immature, or even overly demanding sexually. Sadly, both of them will continue to have less fulfilling sex encounters if such a man has a spouse who enjoys being sexually domineering.

This needless miscommunication between partners can be avoided by being clear with your partner about what you want in bed. If you communicate your needs and desires to your partner, they will be fully aware of your sexual preferences. "Squeeze me harder," "Go slower, baby," "Fuck this pussy like you own it," or "Rub my balls gently" are a few examples.

I'll advise you to concentrate on your desires rather than your distastes. When telling your partner to stop doing something during foreplay or intercourse, use gentleness. Saying "I don't like what you are doing," or "Stop it!" is not appropriate in situations where your partner is giving you oral therapy and you are uncomfortable with the way they are doing it. Say something like, "You're tickling me. Would you mind moving a little more slowly with that warm, lovely tongue of yours?" or "That tickles a lot, baby." Let's give it another go. When expressing your disapproval through nonverbal cues, remember to be tactful. Don't, for instance, yank your partner's hand or yank their tongue off of any part of your body. Keep in mind that they are making every effort to win your approval. You risk upsetting their ego if you express your disapproval of them without tact.

Expressing your desires to your partner requires skillful and compassionate communication. Assisting your partner in providing you with the kind of sexual pleasure and happiness you desire is the aim.

## Dirty Talk Inspiration: Where To Find The Juiciest Ideas

You've reached a brick wall and are at a loss for interesting conversation topics. Take it easy, my love. You can find some x-rated inspiration from other sources if Cosmo and Glamour don't cut it. Here are some surprising locations to check out:

Porn

Let's begin with the most apparent. Although porn isn't for everyone, it's unquestionably a treasure trove of topics for a nasty chat. Pay close attention to the performers' words and delivery. Pay attention to the precise terms and expressions they employ, as well as the timbre and intonation of their voice. This might help you understand the kinds of activities you and your spouse might find enjoyable in the bedroom.

But it's crucial to remember that not everything you see in porn is appealing or even realistic. Make your own decisions, and don't always believe what you see. Something may not always work for you and your partner in real life, even if it works for a performer on film.

My experience: I was first apprehensive to even think of drawing inspiration for dirty discourse from porn. But I decided to give it a shot after hearing so many others rave about it.

I listened carefully to what some of my favorite performers were saying and how they were saying it while I watched them perform. To my surprise, several of their phrases made me feel attracted to them. These were some scorching, steamy lines, and I mentally noted them, even jotting them down in a journal for later.

Of course, I wanted to use my own words and approach, not exactly copy the artists. However, this source of inspiration gave me the confidence to start talking nasty and helped me get started.

Several well-known porn celebrities, such as Riley Reid, Joanna Angel, Tori Black, and Rachel Starr, are well-known for their lewd remarks. These actors are renowned for their ability to get a little dirty on screen and talk a big game.

Words like "Oh yeah, just like that," "Fuck me harder," and "I want to feel you inside me" are frequently used in pornographic films. Naturally, each film and artist is unique, so don't hesitate to jot down any additional words that grab your attention.

Thus, don't be scared to give porn a try if you're feeling stuck and don't know what to say. In the bedroom, you can discover that it inspires creativity and gives you a distinct voice.

erotic books

Look no further than the seductive pages of erotic novels for literary inspiration to boost your game of dirty language! These enticing stories are filled with explicit language and in-depth details about a ton of intense action.

Allow your imagination to go wild by submerging yourself in the world of erotic fiction. Note any phrases or terms that pique your interest and try them in the bedroom, along with your other body parts. You may be surprised to learn how much you love to portray the seductive lead character.

Remember that sexual novels are beautiful because they may be found in a wide variety of genres and styles. There's a book for everyone, regardless of whether they enjoy romance, BDSM, or something else entirely. So prepare to expand your vocabulary of nasty talk by curling up with your favorite sexy book.

Here are a few great erotic novels to get you started if you're looking for some specific recommendations:

Anaïs Nin's collection of sensual short stories, "Delta of Venus," explores themes of power and desire via Nin's distinctive lush and poetic style.

E.L. James' "Fifty Shades of Grey" - Whether you like it or not, this BDSM romance trilogy hugely influences popular culture. The entertaining conversation between Christian and Ana might just inspire you.

Pauline Réage's "The Story of O" This book, a contentious classic of BDSM erotica, follows the subservient O as she makes her way through a society that values severe sexual subjugation and objectification.

Henry Miller's "Tropic of Cancer" This semi-autobiographical novel is well-known for examining the connection between sex and creativity and for its frank portrayals of sexual encounters.

Now, pick out one of these sultry books and begin making notes on the words and phrases that grab your attention!

Soundtrack

When it comes to setting the mood and incorporating some sensual words into your bedroom vocabulary, music truly is a game-changer. There is a musical style to suit every taste, ranging from mellow, seductive ballads to energetic, throbbing dance tracks.

Perhaps it's the way the singer croons about the body of a lover or the raucous innuendos tucked inside the lyrics. Whatever it is, make your own hotlines by using them as a starting point.

Additionally, don't be scared to consider musical genres other than your own. You may be shocked to discover sources of inspiration for nasty conversations in unlikely places. There is bound to be a song that lifts your spirits, whether it be an intense rock anthem, a sensual jazz composition, or an alluring R&B single.

If you want to learn how to talk dirty, I suggest listening to Nicki Minaj. She is a fantastic musician to listen to for inspiration because of her lyrics, renowned for being frank and unapologetic. I turned on some Nicki Minaj one night with my boyfriend to see what nasty jokes we could come up with. We underlined the words and phrases that truly drew our attention as we listened to her lyrics. Some of those lines found their way into our dirty conversation, which was a major turn-on for us both. Thus, listen to Nicki Minaj if you're searching for musical ideas to liven up your conversations in bed!

Time is of the essence.

"Talking about sex right before or right after sex may feel more natural," the FPA notes, "but when neither of you is in a rush, talking without clothes in the heat of the moment can make you feel vulnerable."

That's untrue when it comes to discussing your fantasies about sex; according to Lehmiller, this is best done when you're already feeling energized. When you're aroused, your revulsion reflex lessens, which makes your spouse more amenable. Break the ice by finding something to get the conversation going, like wine or an adult film.

Accept accountability for your enjoyment.

"In couples therapy, one of the most effective exercises I do is to ask couples to step back and just focus on their pleasure and not their partner's," Campbell explains. By doing so, they are spared the thought, 'I have to please this individual.' It gets rid of stage fright, which is annoying. When they start communicating, they have a lot more knowledge to impart, which is transforming.

She claims that when you accept your experience in this way, it is more difficult to criticize the other person. Woodbridge concurs, saying, "People believe they can make someone else cum, but they don't. No one can 'don't' or 'give you an orgasm' when you accept responsibility for your orgasm. It will be more difficult to place the blame that way.

Be precise and explain.

Your spouse cannot read your mind: Tell him if you don't feel like having sex because you just finished a cup of coffee and your breath smells horrible, or you just went to the restroom, and you feel unclean, Campbell said. In the absence of this, she says, "a question I often ask couples in therapy is how do you handle the no and how do you deliver the no?" They will feel rejected and not understand why they are expelled.

Be upbeat rather than judgmental.

Instead of "you," try using "I" statements, suggests Zoë Bailie of The Mix, a nonprofit that helps people under 25. It gives you more control and is less accusing. 'I feel...' instead of 'You make me feel...'." Campbell concurs: treat your partner with kindness. "Say, 'I like it when...' instead of 'stop.'"

Before you say something negative, always offer something nice, like something your spouse did that you like, and advise the FPA. (this goes for non-sexual interactions too).

Woodbridge adds, "I refer to it as 'Facts, Feelings, and Fair Demand.'" 'I observed you like...' or 'I feel like...' is what I mean. Rather than being boring, it provides the other person with constructive criticism." Express your happiness aloud; often, a simple "that was good - let's do it again" may suffice to start a conversation.

As you listen, make inquiries.

According to Campbell, the largest issue with communication is not that people are unable to speak but rather that they are unable to listen. "They're so preoccupied with how to avoid hurting themselves or the other person that they spend all their time thinking about what to say next instead of listening."

How can it be accomplished? Try to appear interested, aloof, and present while putting your emotional reaction on hold, advises Woodbridge. "Tell your partner, 'Tell me more about it.'"

Put yourself in their position, she advises. And you need to make an effort to believe what you hear. We believe our reality is the only one, and other people's perspectives are incorrect. She claims that if you fix it, having those difficult talks will get much easier. .. We have a small favor to ask of you. Millions of people go to the Guardian daily for unbiased, high-quality news, and readers in 180 countries now provide us with financial support.

We, therefore, decided to maintain our reporting accessible to all readers, irrespective of their location or financial situation. This implies that more individuals will be enlightened, unified, and motivated to take significant action. A global journalistic organization like the Guardian that seeks the truth is crucial in these dangerous times. What sets us apart is that we don't have rich owners or stockholders, which meansneither political nor commercial influence can sway our journalism. It is more crucial than ever that we can examine, confront, and expose people in positions of authority with impunity, thanks to our independence.

Regardless of your schedules or time zones, sexting is a terrific way to break the ice and let your partner know you're thinking about them at different times of the day.

Notifying your spouse about what you want them to do while you are out with friends or at work can also offer a sense of excitement and spontaneity. Sexting tips:

The timing is crucial; ascertain their actions before following through. Begin slowly: Like regular sex, sexting is all about the buildup. Give an example: Don't hesitate to mention EVERY detail. Recall to relive prior private moments that you have shared.

Naturally, you can always take a deep breath and state up front that you've got some ideas you'd like to contribute. According to licensed clinical therapist Jared M. Grant, PsyD, "sometimes it's just easier to get it out there," Bustle was informed. Gather your ideas after that so you can introduce the topic of discussion with a few targeted queries, worries, etc. Grant suggests that you might even want to schedule an opportunity to speak to make it seem less abrupt. For instance, you probably shouldn't bring up the topic if you're upset, exhausted, or running late for work. Instead, schedule a time to relax, talk, and sit down on the couch.

Grant advises starting the conversation by explaining to your partner why you haven't shared these things with them and making it obvious that it won't be negative. Rather, acknowledge that discussing sex has occasionally been taboo. According to Grant, there's a good chance they'll feel the same way and value the haven you're providing for them to be vulnerable. Inform your lover the next time something sexy occurs, and you're into it. Grant is right when discussing your interests; it will lead to more of the same. "People like to be good at things," according to him. "Tell them when they are and see how it happens more often."

## Tips For Tantric Intimacy

Examining this age-old spiritual practice helps you transcend ordinary consciousness and join with the divine, as well as introducing you and your partner to full-body orgasms. Here are some pointers for enjoying tantric sex to the fullest.

Make a routine. Just like with anything important, you need to set up time for tantric pleasure. You must choose a time of day when you are free to perform the tantric sex rituals, as they cannot be completed quickly. To reap the long-term advantages of tantric sex, you will need to engage in the practice at least once a week if you wish to make it a habit. Create a tantric sex timetable that works for both of you and your lover without any constraints. Tantric sex is best done in the morning when it's fresh and energizing for the day.

Knowing this will help you approach tantric sex with a playful attitude. Give your spouse complete freedom to express themselves and accept their desires even if they initially seem strange. You could, for example, make variations of kissing where you suck on each other's extended tongues as if they were candies rather than kissing intensely. However, you must be creative only to the extent that each of you is prepared and eager to contribute to the other.

Prepare your area; when the mood is off, it might be hard to get emotional and mental clarity. First, you should stop any distracting noises, either external or internal. After that, decorate your room with lovely, eye-catching items. You can place vases on the floor and apply perfume and incense on your clothing to arouse your senses. It will be much simpler to transcend the mundane plane of life and unite with the divine when you're in the correct frame of mind.

Use music and lighting to create a conducive atmosphere. You don't need to spend much money on fancy lighting fixtures, but everything is possible if you use your imagination. Adding candles to your room will make it look amazing.

Additionally, a well-chosen playlist can improve the atmosphere, but you should confirm that your significant other shares your taste in music. Make sure the room temperature is correct as well. You can change the temperature in your room or open your windows if it's too hot outside. A setting that perfectly combines soothing music and lighting allows people to find peace more quickly.

Have a bath; it will convey a negative opinion of you, so the last thing you want to do is come up unclean. Therefore, instead of taking a fast shower that can leave dirt stuck to some regions of your body, you might take a long, relaxing bath. Bath time is essential because it helps you both unwind.

Engage in physical activity; a little body shake helps release tension in the surrounding tissues. Your body may develop tensions around important body components due to sickness and stress that have built up. Thus, you tend to alleviate your body's tissues and enable optimal bodily function when you shake your body a little. Engage in gentle movements to improve your ability to shake your head, neck, shoulders, and hands. You will feel more pleasure whether you do these exercises individually or in a group.

Meditate; simply being in a supportive setting is insufficient. To reach a high level of being, your mind must be active. The chatter in your head reduces when you meditate. Learning to breathe in harmony is one of the main components of meditation. Just choose a peaceful spot and begin to pay attention to your breath. It's helpful to support yourself by placing your palm on your chest, but the most crucial thing is to be aware of your breathing pattern. Holding hands together during a meditation can lead to heightened closeness. Continue until your energies blend and you become present.

Flatter your relationship. By using flattery, you can increase your partner's trust and freedom. Tell them something about them that you think is admirable or fascinating. Their personality, physical characteristics, or other skills can be the cause. Flattery could work better for you because most people enjoy feeling affirmed. However, even as you compliment them, remember to be genuine and avoid coming across as needy. Exercise caution when praising them because you don't want to appear strange or obscene. It will also put a strain on your partner to compliment you.

For some reason, most tantric sex practitioners find that making eye contact is the most difficult element of the process. While it's true that making eye contact can appear unsettling, it's only when you're not doing it perfectly or aren't in the proper frame of mind to ascend to a higher dimension of existence. Making eye contact is essential to bringing energies together. You must learn to make meaningful eye contact since your spouse represents the divine, and your objective is to integrate with the divine. It will feel amazing to connect with your partner, and you could wish to coordinate your breathing to heighten your senses.

One of the most beloved positions for developing a close, personal connection with your lover is to sit with your legs around them. The female partner sits down and wraps her legs around her male companion, who is seated cross-legged. Subsequently, they embrace each other, pressing their bodies together and establishing a coordinated breathing pattern. The partners should conduct this technique in their undies for maximum calm. Their bodies meld together, their energies uniting as they breathe. The female inhales when the male exhales, and the male inhales when the female exhales. This strengthens the relationship between the partners.

Investigate your senses; tantric sex provides a way to enhance your emotional and sensory bodies. You can enhance your senses of touch, sight, smell, and sound through tantric sex. You can explore the sensual side by providing your companion with various non-visual stimuli while wearing a blindfold. Play some relaxing music and use touch to stimulate their body. You might use silk and rough material alternately. This will enhance their ability to perceive different materials even when they are not visible. Additionally, you might use different essential oils to arouse their sense of smell.

When it comes to having sex, you might want to proceed cautiously. This will, among other things, give you control over your orgasm and enable you to stay in spiritual awareness without succumbing to sensual cravings. You have to understand that the purpose of tantric sex is primarily spiritual, not sexual, and that, as such, spiritual demands come first. When exploring your partner's body, you must be cautious and gentle, touching and stroking them lightly throughout, pausing sometimes to let them fully enjoy the sensations. Your companion will get so excited that they will titter just before they pass out. By practicing slowing down, you can assist your spouse in being one with the divine and achieving spiritual enlightenment, which is essentially wisdom, peace, and tranquility.

Orgasms involve the entire body; most men only associate orgasms with ejaculating. However, the man's vitality is depleted, and he will have to wait a little while before he can have another orgasm. The man may feel an orgasm throughout his entire body and for a prolonged period if he has a full-body orgasm. Having control over your ejaculation—that is, stopping yourself from ejaculating and instead having an orgasm—is the key to achieving a complete body orgasm. You can then continue to savor yourself. Holding back on your ejaculation will allow your partner to build up to their orgasm. When you're both ready, you'll release your entire body orgasm, combining your energies and assisting you in connecting with the divine spirit.

Conclude with a heartfelt hug and a brief conversation on taking care of yourself after the session. Emotions will run high whether or not sex is involved, and walking away is the worst thing you can do. Your companion will become vulnerable due to the elevated emotions, so you may wish to hug them and initiate a conversation. They'll feel more assured of your devotion and love as a result.

5. Signs to watch out for when irritation starts

Being irrationally angry with the two guardians or the person who moved out is acceptable. Determining how much a young high school student's irritability is related to their separation might be challenging. "Ponder what your kid resembled before the partition and how their behavior or temperaments have changed," Freeman suggests. "That provides some insight with regards to the reason. Nonetheless, regardless of whether you infer that the issue isn't separate from related, that doesn't mean you don't address it."

i. Necessities of parents: Maintaining open lines of communication reduces the chance that serious problems may go unnoticed. Children in this age group can be harder to approach; sometimes, they act as if they'd prefer not to be approached. In any event, most young teenagers crave and truly require their relationships with guardians. "Loads of children have told me, throughout the long term, that they were trying their folks to check whether they truly minded," Freeman asserts. Thus, even when your child seems to be trying to push you away, keep talking; at the very least, include them in the conversation about the things they need to discuss.

ii. Names were modified in response to public demand.

Overcoming the Divide

Three factors, according to research, help children of all ages adjust to life after separation:

Having strong points for a relationship with both parents (whenever circumstances permit and when the child needs it).

Providing excellent basic nurturing (what experts refer to as adhering to the nurturing limit).

Having a negligible openness to struggle. There were no real surprises there. For guardians, the real test is doing it.

Bolstering the connection

Iii. After a separation, a parent-child relationship can be lost if one parent disappears from the child's life or if one parent (or both) undermines the other's bond with the child. Alternatively, the child may very well be the one to retreat, according to Rhonda Freeman, Toronto's Families in Transition administrator. "A few youngsters have a demeanor that makes it hard for them to think about the continuous welcomes, farewells and changes."

These are uncontrollable factors for guardians. In addition to attending to your obligations with a child, you should consider his relationship with the other parent. "Assuming that you stigmatize the other parent before your kids, you are depreciating their relationship," Freeman explains.

## Iv. Excellent care

Maintaining the kind of caring that is normally expected can be challenging when you are grieving over a broken relationship and preoccupied with legal counsel and trials. Make a great effort to keep your interactions with your children and adult matters apart, and if you need help getting assistance, get it from someone else.

Freeman and Californian physician Joan B. Kelly recommend staying apart from parent education programs. "Many guardians think, 'I needn't bother with this,'" says Kelly. To locate classes, check with your local data center, family administration office, attorney, judge, specialist, or advocate. "However, research shows that isolated guardians who separate from training classes are the most certain."

V. Handling conflict

The best action is to stop the separation conflict before it starts. The terrible pain that Janice Weiss* of Calgary experienced when her parents divorced. Mom's House, Dad's House by Isolina Ricci contains advice she and her ex-husband agreed to follow. "I swore my children wouldn't go through that." Here are five ways to lower the heat when the struggle is intense: "It became like a book of scriptures, and it truly helped."

• Keep conversations to a minimum when switching the children. Follow the basics, such as confirming the times for collection and drop-off.

• Aim to avoid using children to communicate with your former partner.

• Exchange important nuances that are written down in paper copy. Some parents use email, while others use a book that has the children travel this way and that. If matters become heated, have someone else—a teacher, mediator, or friend—check your email for offensive language before sending it.

- Take note of the other parent's interactions with the children. Arrive on time for pickups or have the kids ready. Ensure everything they need to bring (school supplies, clothing, unique hardware) is also ready.
- Think about your former accomplice's safety. Right now, you have a different kind of relationship; nothing stops you from joining a business-oriented group. You don't need to know as much about their personal life as you used to.

Our daily lives are lived in a reality where the answers to almost all our questions are at our fingertips.

How amazing is that?

We can ask almost any question and receive an answer in seconds by simply picking up our phone or sitting at a computer. Furthermore, as guardians, very few people have more to gain from instant access to data than us.

AN ESSENTIAL FACTOR OF HUMAN INTERACTION IS RAPPORT.

The important thing is to build a rapport.

I think I may have told you how important communication is.

93% of communication is nonverbal, with only 7% occurring verbally.

This suggests that our words influence others only 7% of the time we speak.

Rapport is one way that communication can manifest.

It entails conversing to foster closer intimacy.

You should pay more attention to HOW you say things than WHAT you say when trying to build rapport with a woman.

There are three effective strategies to build a connection with a lady through matching and mirroring.

You should mimic and replicate three things: your tone, your breathing pattern, and your posture.

A. Place.

What is the other person doing with her hands during your conversation?

Is she slouching, or is she sitting upright?

Does she tilt in your direction or away from it?

If she's slouching, you probably shouldn't sit up straight.

If she is displaying comfort and curiosity, lean into her.

Take note of how a woman stands and moves, then try to mimic her.

When you copy her, exercise caution.

If she does, take your time running your hands through her hair. You shouldn't be able to get away with imitating her.

Your goal is to synchronize your motions to make you appear cohesive to a woman.

We are naturally drawn to those who are similar to us. Mirroring makes this clear.

2. A FLOWING RHYTHM.

One of the greatest ways to connect with a lady is to breathe in harmony.

In sync with her respiration.

This is strengthening your relationship.

This also applies to the volume and speed at which your discussion partner speaks.

If she's talking reasonably calmly and slowly, it wouldn't make sense for you to speak hastily.

Observe how she is breathing.

Does she breathe briefly from her chest or deeply from her diaphragm?

Observe her actions and attempt to integrate them into your breathing technique.

3. SET YOUR ENERGY LEVEL IN LINE WITH HER VOICE.

We must mimic a woman's excitement and tone to build rapport.

A situation's general demeanor or attitude is referred to as its tone.

If the female speaks softly, it makes more sense for you to mimic her voice rather than trying to dominate her with a loud one.

This is considerate and demonstrates empathy and comfort to the other person.

This is the most effective way to build rapport. The way you express something matters more than what you say.

If something is horrific and said in jest or with sarcasm, the entire meaning of the sentence changes.

But the message will likewise be bad if something horrible is uttered with conviction.

For example, if you said, "I hate you!" or "I hate you," she would respond angrily or ironically.

Since tone is key, practice modifying your daily discussions' tone and tempo.

Because you've had practice, it will consequently be much easier for you to get close to a girl you adore.

Furthermore, if the other person in the conversation is introverted, it would be useless to seem extroverted.

You try to put her at ease by showing her how much you are alike.

Highlighting how your communication styles are similar is the best way to show how similar you are.

Alright, you're well on your way to developing a deep and meaningful relationship with any woman you desire. This is how you build rapport and, eventually, attraction with a woman by establishing trust and a feeling of similarity.

Nonverbal Clues and Body Language

Nonverbal cues and body language are crucial components of communication and greatly impact how people receive and understand information. These cues can communicate attitudes, intentions, and feelings that words alone might not be able to represent.

Nonverbal cues: their significance in communication

Facial expressions are among the most significant nonverbal clues. Expressions on the face can convey a person's feelings, including fear, anger, grief, and happiness. They may also reveal a person's degree of interest in a subject or degree of participation in a conversation. A lady is probably interested and engaged in the conversation if, for instance, she is grinning and making eye contact. However, if a lady is frowning or turning her head away, it could mean she is disengaged or not interested in the conversation.

One further significant nonverbal clue is body position. One's attitude, emotions, and degree of confidence can all be inferred from their posture. A lady is probably feeling confident and forceful if, for instance, she is sitting up straight with her shoulders back. However, if a lady is hunching over or crossing her arms, it could mean she's uncomfortable or defensive.

Another crucial nonverbal cue is gestures. They can be used to express emotions or highlight a point; for example, pointing can be used to highlight a point, or shrugging can be used to show uncertainty. A woman probably agrees with what is being said if, for instance, she nods her head while listening. However, it's more likely that a woman disagrees if she shakes her head or displays a disapproving expression.

And last, voice tone is a crucial nonverbal cue. It might reflect a person's degree of confidence, assertiveness, or defensiveness, as well as emotions like happiness, sadness, rage, or fear. For instance, when a lady speaks in a low, soft tone, it could be a sign that she's nervous or uncomfortable. Conversely, a lady may feel confident and forceful if she speaks in a strong, assertive tone.

In summary, nonverbal cues and body language are crucial components of communication and greatly impact how others receive and understand messages. Men can better understand women and prevent miscommunication by being aware of and comprehending nonverbal clues. To guarantee a smooth and productive connection, men should be aware of their body language, tone of voice, gestures, and facial expressions.

## 19. Sex and Sexuality

Instruct your daughter to respect her body and herself and talk about sex within the framework of a caring, wholesome relationship. "Children learn about sex from birth by witnessing the people around them," according to one researcher.

Lavender gives voice to herself. "Rather of focusing on the act of sex, you can establish the framework for a healthy attitude toward her body and the value of sharing it with someone who cares for and respects her when she is older."

## 20. Privacy on the Internet and in Person

Respecting your daughter's privacy is important, but you must also consider her social and physical health. Teach her the definition of social media responsibility in words she can comprehend: anything posted online, including pictures and personal information about herself, can be viewed by anybody at any time. Limit her screen time and follow her on social media to see who she's talking to and what she publishes.

## 21. Take Good Care Of Yourself And Protect It

Teach your daughters to ask for help from adults they can trust in times of need. For instance, if they are being bullied, they should know who to tell and how to tell adults they can trust, and they should feel confident in saying "no" when appropriate.

## 22. Teach Her How To Be Kind And Respectful To Others

Encourage your daughter to recognize the inner beauty in others, just as you would like her to feel good about herself. That is the well-known Golden Rule. Instill your daughter the value of treating people how she would like to be treated.

To help you teach your daughter about her body, many wonderful resources are available, from books and websites like Kids Health to her pediatrician and teachers. Place a book suitable for her age on her bed and watch her response.

Taking an active interest in her life and showing her that you care will make talking about subjects like her body more comfortable and natural.

The accentuation of consent is another fundamental viewpoint. Women are expected to learn about their rights and the importance of consent in sexual relationships through extensive sexual education. It highlights the importance of clear communication, mutual respect, and boundaries. Sexual education can help prevent sexual violence, compulsion, and unfavorable power dynamics by fostering a culture of consent.

In addition, extensive sexual education supports a broad and diverse approach that recognizes the many experiences, personalities, and orientations of women. It includes dispelling stereotypes, reducing barriers to entry, and promoting acceptance and dignity for individuals of all sexual orientations and directions.

In general, this section emphasizes the need for comprehensive sexual education that addresses women's sexual pleasure, consent, and well-being.

**Breaking Barriers:** Comprehensive sexual education aims to disentangle cultural barriers and constraints, including discussions about women's sexual pleasure and well-being. It helps to normalize conversations and advance a greater understanding of women's sexuality by openly addressing these issues.

**Body Inspiration and Self-Acknowledgment:** Women who receive this kind of sexual education feel more empowered and self-aware. It emphasizes how unique every woman's physique is while standardizing the common types that are out there. Women can improve their relationships with their bodies and their sex lives by developing a positive self-perception.

**Strong Links:** Comprehensive sexual education emphasizes the value of strong bonds and interpersonal skills. It educates women on how to set boundaries, recognize warning signs of unwelcome relationships, and advocate for their needs and desires in safe spaces.

Strengthening and Office: Providing women with comprehensive sexual education equips them with the knowledge and tools necessary to make educated decisions about their sexual lives. It gives women more agency and self-determination by enabling them to express their desires, make decisions based on informed consent, and safely experiment with sexuality.

Taking Care of Fantasies and Misinterpretations: Total sexual education issues, common myths, and incorrect assessments on women's sexual health. It dispels misconceptions that could harm women's sexual prosperity by providing accurate information on topics including contraception, menstruation, sexual pleasure, and fruitfulness.

**Integration of LGBTQ+ Encounters:** A comprehensive approach to sexual education views and considers the experiences of those who identify as LGBTQ+. It acknowledges many sexual orientations and directions and provides information and support that is all-inclusive and relevant to women regardless of their sexual orientation or personality.

**Assent Education:** Providing assent education is a crucial component of comprehensive sexual education. It teaches women the value of purposeful, enthusiastic, and ongoing consent during sexual interactions. It also addresses topics of assault culture, sexual compulsion, and the need to set boundaries and value personal autonomy.

These elements can be included in sexual education programs so that society can address women's sexual pleasure, consent, and well-being in a more thorough, knowledgeable, and supportive manner.

6. Do you think masturbating is unhealthy?

Although it can be one of the most awkward subjects to bring up with your adolescent, talking to them about masturbation is an essential first step in identifying their normal sexual development.

Furthermore, it creates a "sex-positive" atmosphere at home, which may defer having a first sexual experience and lower subsequent risk-taking.

Talking to your children about masturbation is another way to have a conversation with them about sex. Instead of talking about their sexual interactions with other people, you have a personal conversation with them about developing a healthy sexual identity. Talking to kids going through puberty about touchy themes like masturbation can help them feel less guilty and ashamed of their changing bodies.

It's important to talk about masturbation because

It encourages body awareness and autonomy.

It allows people to enjoy themselves freely.

It shows them you are willing to be honest and vulnerable with them in difficult situations.

It illustrates how to address adult subjects with empathy and curiosity.

Talking with your child about consent and sexting, for example, is a lot easier now that you've started the conversation about these important boundaries.

When You Witness Them "In the Act," What Should You Do?

When the dreaded moment arrives, and you see your child masturbating "in the act," don't freak out.

Take a big breath, give yourself and your child a break, and wait before responding to your teen's masturbation. Your responses can permanently influence teens' perceptions of their own bodies' reactions to sexual arousal.

If you witness your adolescent engaging in excessive grooming, take the following action:

Express your heartfelt regrets for any invasion of privacy, such as when you entered a room without knocking first.

Acknowledge that it was a mistake to ignore this spatial restriction.

Think about your reactions to your child's behavior and what they say about your views about masturbation and sex. Take your time and place when doing this. You can justify your "effort" if you're disgusted or guilty.

Make it clear that this is not a decision they can make when you tell them you want to talk with them about what happened at a time that works for them.

## The Fundamentals Of Sexual Education

1. Don't assume anything

Don't assume that young people have heard or know everything because everything seems to occur quickly. Sexuality is vitally important, and our kids should be taught the facts about it in a way that is both obvious and imbued with the values of respect for others and self-preservation. This means that before we can fully appreciate the beauty of love relationships and their potential for manipulation or exploitation, we must first grasp how our bodies function.

Never assume that someone is taking any action just because a question is posed. Many kids may inquire about sexuality, sex, contraception, and other subjects out of pure curiosity or in response to something they have heard. Young people ask questions to get trustworthy answers or clarification. They need to gather precise data. A conversation can be sparked by providing information.

Never presume that kids understand what we've spoken to them or that we understand all they're trying to say. Teens should always be asked to repeat what they have heard (and vice versa).

If something is unclear, ask for more clarification and be ready to restate or reword information to make it easier to understand.

2. Provide reasons rather than lectures.

We need to support our children in being capable of independent, reasoned decision-making. We risk pushing them away from us and sometimes even toward the habits we detest when we boss them about or give them an emotional lecture complete with dire threats.

Lecture failure can be attributed to two basic factors. They are often unnecessarily abstract in the first place because they provide complicated connections between a sequence of events and a terrible outcome. Second, young children hear the anger and sense the horror without ever benefiting from the concepts because adults often lecture in difficult situations.

We might discover new ways to deliver the same information so that our teenagers can consider it carefully and use it to form their judgments. When young people solve problems independently (even with our assistance!), they are more inclined to accept the ideas and answers as their own.

Start by having talks rather than imposing demands. Tell your children that you're educating them to make good decisions by having conversations with them. When we place demands on teenagers, they may revolt.

However, when they know that we are trying to keep them safe and moral, they respect our guidance and the boundaries we set for them.

Make certain that your children comprehend the rationale behind your needs when it comes to sexual activity. Your teens will understand why engaging in particular activities will support their health, as well as your views and values on sexuality.

Talk to kids about sex, not just as part of a safety message but also in the context of relationships in general. That will also help them understand why you are giving them advice. Because of this, they won't feel like you're manipulating them, and they'll understand that you want to lead and protect them.

The positive aspect of being naughty

How can I make my relationships and sex life better with dirty talk?

First, let's talk about the most evident benefit: Sex is made even hotter by lewd conversation. The key to successful sex is honest communication. A person's conscience is a sensitive organ. The worst possible thing that may happen during a sexual encounter is to make a recommendation and then have it misinterpreted afterward. With dirty talk, you and your partner can express your desires and provide constructive criticism non-aggressively.

Examine this statement:

Woman: "At this moment, do not come. Allow me to go first this time."

Sincere? Yes, in fact.

Beneficial? Indeed.

Conciliatory? Not really.

Attractive? Without a doubt.

Although the woman's intention is admirable, a guy will likely feel as though a) she is criticizing his manner or b) she is accusing him of being conceited.

c) She feels that he doesn't understand what he is doing because she is showing him how to have sex; d) She is far from peaking, meaning that all of his hard work has been in vain.

Here's the truth: Any words spoken during sexual activity have the potential to interrupt bliss; therefore, even if they may cause discomfort, make sure your statements are warranted before making them.

Now, examine this input's "naughty" version:

"Goodness, child, continue doing that, and I'm going to come soon..."

Notice the difference? Giving instructions while doing the task could discourage, distract, and break the partner's mindset. However, in the unlikely event that you alter each other's comments and turn them into seductive conversation, it will motivate your partner to perform better in the bedroom. When you can tell your partner where, when, and how you need things without hurting his inner self, how can it not lead to raunchy sex?

IN BED, DIRTY TALK SUPPORTS YOUR MATE'S TRUST.

Dirty language has the power to transform shy women into body queens and a lover into an alpha male—not terrific, but alpha. If you're in dire need of amazing sex, then take it upon yourself to create the ideal version of your partner. Women who are overly self-conscious about their bodies are hesitant to agree to strong room fantasies such as striptease or trying sex locations that make them feel overly exposed.

Having a positive self-image is essential for amazing sex. Whenever someone sees someone irritating in the mirror, the notion automatically finds its way into their subconscious, which naturally diminishes their charisma. In this way, one finds it difficult to be thrilled no matter how attractive his partner is. In other words, for your partner to turn you on, you must first turn someone else on.

Men may experience strain and stress related to execution due to unforeseen circumstances, their grit, penis size, and other factors. Some men may seem confident on the outside, but in reality, they are uneasy about ceding control of the situation. As a result, individuals could be afraid of being bound or nervous about someone touching their areolas.

Use obscene conversation to compliment your woman's flawless figure or to assure your boyfriend of his prowess in bed.

Model's response: "I love running my tongue over your bends."

"It's wonderful how your bosoms bob when you proceed onward top of me."

"I love the wonderful way your cockerel fills me."

It maintains alignment between you and your partner. A delightful aspect of naughty chat in bed is that it encourages partners to communicate more verbally rather than leaving it up to them to figure out things like their feelings, thoughts, or where the clit is. While moaning, whispering, and yelling are generally excellent, the problem is that they can easily be confused.

Look into this commonplace scenario:

A young woman yells with delight. Feeling anxious, the fellow pauses his work and inquires, "Did I hurt you?"

Perplexing, huh? That would have been amazing if she had used shady language to let her boyfriend know he was headed in the right direction. Something as simple as "Child, don't stop. "It feels so good" would have been appropriate.

Talking about sex releases creative energy and romantic feelings.

It's never good for couples when things get tiresome in between the covers. The thing about the lewd conversation is that it awakens a fearless, creative, and intensely sensual aspect of you. Effectively, words turn into actions. Perhaps all you have to say regarding sensuous vocabulary right now is, "Goodness God, I'm coming." But within seconds, you'll be saying things like, "I'm going to come over to your office, close the blinds, strap you to the chair, and lick you until you beg me to screw you." When you speak these words for everyone to hear, they are incorporated into your and your lover's subconscious. This dream scenario takes shape in your mind and will continue to recur. You will soon pay him/her a visit at work with a few ties in your pocket.

www.ingramcontent.com/pod-product-compliance
Lightning Source LLC
Chambersburg PA
CBHW052141110526
44591CB00012B/1816